Contents

What Is a Snake?

Snakes are reptiles. All snakes are **cold-blooded**. They do not have arms, legs, or eyelids. Snakes move in different ways. All snakes use their muscles and scales to move. There are snakes all over the world, except Antarctica. There are more than 3,000 different kinds of snakes. Snakes are **carnivores**. Some people think snakes are scary and dangerous. Most snakes are not dangerous at all. They help keep pests, like rats and mice away from houses and barns.

SNAKE BITE

A snake's jaw can **unhinge**. All snakes swallow their prey whole.

PREHISTORIC SNAKES

Snakes have been on Earth for more than 100 million years. Snake **fossils** are very hard to find.

One of the biggest snakes ever was Titanoboa (say it like this: Tie-TAN-oh-bow-uh). It was 48 feet (14.6 m) long! That is longer than a school bus! It weighed more than a ton. Titanoboa lived about 58 millions years ago. That was a few million years after the dinosaurs were **extinct**.

SNAKE BITE

Snakes shed their skin about three times each year.

1 TON

Fangs!

Most snakes have teeth. There are four rows on top and two on the bottom. Only **venomous** snakes have fangs. Fangs are sharp, long, and **hollow** teeth, like a needle. These are connected to a sac in the snake's head. The sac makes a liquid called **venom**. When a snake bites, it releases this **venom**. **Venom** is used to kill its prey.

In some **venomous** snakes, the fangs fold back into the mouth. This keeps them from biting themselves.

snakes with the longest fangs
(shown actual size):

Gaboon viper – The gaboon viper has the longest fangs of any snake. They can be up to 2-inches (5-cm) long.

Rattlesnake – It depends on the size of the rattlesnake. Their fangs can be 1-inch (2.5-cm) long.

Cobra — The longest venomous snake in the world has small fangs that are 1/4-inch (.6-cm) long.

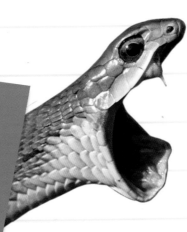

SNAKE BITE

Baby snakes can be very dangerous. They do not know how much **venom** to **inject**. They **inject** a lot! WARNING! Never go near a snake in the wild.

Boomslang — This snake has rear fangs set toward the front of the mouth in several rows. They are about 1/8-inch (.3-cm) long.

SNAKE BITE

Snakes have a forked tongue that they use to smell. They also feel vibrations through the ground.

VENOMOUS VS POISONOUS

Think about it like this: some snakes are **venomous**. They **inject venom** into their prey. If a snake was **POISONOUS**, you would have to eat it for it to make you sick.

Top 10 Most Dangerous Snakes

Ranking based on average size of snake, amount of venom in each bite, toxicity of venom, length of fangs, and aggressive behavior.

 **10** **Rattlesnake**
Rattlesnakes don't always rattle before they strike. They don't always strike every time they rattle.

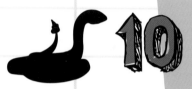 **9** **Death Adder**
It is called a death adder because it strikes as soon as it is alarmed.

 **8** **Taipan**
It is believed that the Inland Taipan is the most **venomous snake** in the world.

 **7** **Tiger Snake**
Its **toxic venom** and aggressive behavior make this a dangerous snake.

Cobra

6 Cobras can stand as tall as one third of their body length. An 18-foot (5.5 m) King Cobra can look a full-grown man in the eyes!

Blue Krait

5 When a Krait bites, it holds on and **injects** a lot of **venom**.

Eastern Brown Snake

4 The eastern brown snake has a bad temper and is aggressive. It is also very useful to farmers. It helps control the number of rats and mice.

Saw-scaled Viper

3 Saw-scaled vipers strike quickly with a lot of **venom.**

Black Mamba

2 Black mambas will strike with lightning speed and many times.

Russell's Viper

1 Russell's viper can strike from 5 feet (1.5 m) away.

Rattlesnake

- There are 24 different kinds of rattlesnakes, including the eastern and western diamondbacks, sidewinder, and pygmy.

- All rattlesnakes have a rattle at the tip of their tail.

- The rattles are made of the same material as your fingernails.

- Rattlesnakes eat once every two weeks or so.

SNAKE FAST FACTS

Length: 1 foot to 8 feet (.3 m to 2.4 m), depending on the species. The eastern diamondback is the longest.

Food: Mice, rats, squirrels, rabbits, and even some birds

Found: North, Central, and South Americas

A rattlesnake has a hollow spot between the eyes and nostrils called a **pit**. That is why they are called **pit** vipers.

Latin name: *Crotalus*
(Say it like this: CROW-tal-uss)

9

Death Adder

- Death adders spend their day curled up in loose soil or fallen leaves.

- A death adder is very sneaky. It lies in leaves to camouflage itself and waits for its prey.

- The death adder's **venom** is very **toxic.**

- Death adders are light brown, orange, and yellow, with dark brown stripes.

- Death adder's can swim too!

SNAKE FAST FACTS
Length: Average 27 to 39 inches (69 to 99 cm)
Food: Rodents, lizards, and birds
Found: Australia

SNAKE BITE

The death adder has a "lure" on its tail to attract prey, just like when you go fishing.

atin name: *Acanthophis antarcticus*
(ay it like this: ah-CAN-thow-fiss ant-ARC-ti-cuss)

11

Taipan

- There are two kinds of Taipans: the inland and coastal.

- Taipans are yellow in color, but their skin changes color with the seasons.

- The inland taipan is a shy snake, but the coastal taipan is very aggressive.

- These snakes are extremely fast and can instantly and accurately strike multiple times.

- Taipans are most active in the early morning or in the afternoon when it is cooler.

- The Inland Taipan has fangs that are ⅛-inch (.3-cm) to ¼-inch long (.6-cm).

SNAKE FAST FACTS

Length: 6 feet to 10 feet (1.8 m to 3 m)

Food: Rodents, small mammals, and birds

Found: Australia

SNAKE BITE

The **venom** in one bite from an inland taipan is enough to kill 250,000 mice. They eat only one at time.

Latin name: *Oxyuranus*
(say it like this: ox-EE-yur-ah-nuss)

13

Tiger Snake

- Tiger snakes range in color from dark olive brown to dark brown with off-white or yellow bands.

- Tiger snakes can climb very well.

- These snakes prefer being near water.

- Tiger snake fangs are 1/8-inch (.3-cm) to 1/4-inch (.6-cm) long.

SNAKE FAST FACTS

Length: 4 feet to 6.5 feet (1.2 m to 2 m)

Food: Fish, frogs, tadpoles, lizards, birds, mammals, other snakes, and **carrion**

Found: Australia

14

A cornered Tiger Snake will hiss loudly as it **inflates and deflates** its body.

Latin name: *Notechis scutatus*
(say it like this: NOTE-ih-kiss SKU-tah-tuss)

15

Cobra

- All cobras have the famous hood at their necks.
- The number of cobra species range from 28 to 270 depending on how you define a cobra.
- Cobras can raise the upper part of their bodies.
- Cobras have round pupils and smooth scales.
- Cobras vary in color from red to yellow and black to mottled or banded.
- King cobras are considered the most intelligent snakes in the world.
- Spitting cobras can spit **venom** as well as **inject venom.** They can spit up to 6 feet (1.8 m) away with perfect aim into the eyes of their prey.
- Hooding happens when a snake spreads out its neck ribs forming a wide section of its body near the head.
- Most cobras hunt at dawn and dusk.
- The king cobra is the longest species of **venomous** snake in the world.
- Cobras can go days or even months without feeding.

SNAKE FAST FACTS

Length: 4 feet to 18 feet (1.2 m to 5.5 m), depending on the species

Food: Other snakes, birds, lizards, bird eggs, small mammals, and **carrion**

Found: Africa, Middle East, India, Southeast Asia, and Indonesia

SNAKE BITE

One bite from a king cobra has enough **venom** to kill one elephant, but they don't eat elephants.

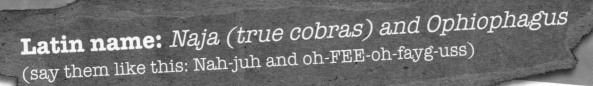

Latin name: *Naja (true cobras) and Ophiophagus*
(say them like this: Nah-juh and oh-FEE-oh-fayg-uss)

17

Blue Krait

 The blue krait has white with black or dark blue bands.

 Blue kraits like water.

 Kraits are one of the world's deadliest snakes.

 During the day, a krait curls its body into a loose ball with its head hidden.

 Blue kraits are not aggressive unless annoyed.

 The blue krait is very active at night.

SNAKE FAST FACTS

Length: 2 feet to 5 feet (.6 m to 1.5 m)

Food: Other snakes, frogs, lizards, and small mammals

Found: Southeast Asia

SNAKE BITE

The bite of the blue krait is painless. You won't even know that you've been bitten.

Latin name: *Bungarus candidus*
(say it like this: bun-GAR-uss can-DEE-duss)

Eastern Brown Snake

- The eastern brown snake is considered to be the second-most **venomous** land snake.

- Eastern brown snakes move very fast.

- Eastern brown snakes vary in color from tan to gray or dark brown with a cream, yellow, or pale-orange belly.

- Eastern brown snakes are found near humans and around farm buildings.

- An eastern brown snake's bite is almost painless.

SNAKE FAST FACTS

Length: Up to 7.8 feet (2.4 m)

Food: Frogs, reptiles, reptile eggs, birds, mice, and rats

Found: Australia

The fangs of an eastern brown snake are about 1/8-inch (.3 cm).

Latin name: *Pseudonaja textilis*
(say it like this: sue-DOH-nah-jah tex-TILL-iss)

21

Saw-scaled Viper

- There are eight species of saw-scaled vipers.

- Saw-scaled vipers are small and bad tempered.

- They are very aggressive at night.

- Saw-scaled vipers move in a sidewinding motion.

- The saw-scaled viper has large eyes for hunting at night.

SNAKE FAST FACTS

Length: 1 foot to 3 feet (.3 m to 1 m)

Food: Small mammals, birds, snakes, lizards, frogs, scorpions, and centipedes

Found: Dry regions of Africa, Middle East, Pakistan, India, and Sri Lanka

when threatened, this snake will rub its body together to make a "sizzling" sound.

Latin name: *Echis*
(say it like this: EE-kiss)

23

Black Mamba

- Black mambas are fast, nervous, and very aggressive.

- A black mamba's skin is gray.

- The black mamba is the most-feared snake in Africa.

- Black mambas live in trees.

SNAKE FAST FACTS

Length: 8 feet to 14 feet (2.4 m to 4.3 m)

Food: Rodents, bats, birds, and lizards

Found: Savannas and rocky hills of eastern and southern Africa

SNAKE BITE

The black mamba gets its name from the blue-black color of the inside of its mouth.

Latin name: *Dendroaspis polylepis*
(say it like this: den-DRO-asp-iss pol-EE-lep-iss)

Russell's Viper

 Russell's vipers hunt at night.

 A Russell's viper sits and waits for its prey in thick grasses near farms.

 A Russell's viper has a light brown body with dark-edged brown blotches down its back perfect for camouflage.

SNAKE FAST FACTS

Length: 4 feet to 5.5 feet (1.2 m to 1.7 m)

Food: Rats, mice, shrew, squirrels, land crabs, scorpions, and small lizards

Found: Asia and Southeast Asia

26

SNAKE BITE

The Russell's viper is named after Patrick Russell, a Scottish **herpetologist** from the 1700s.

Latin name: *Daboia*
(say it like this: da-BOY-ee-ah)

Belcher's Sea Snake

- Sea snake **venom** is more dangerous than a cobra or mamba.

- These snakes are not very aggressive.

- The tail of the Belcher's sea snake acts like a paddle helping it swim.

- There are **valves** above the nostrils that stay closed when the snake is underwater.

- Belcher's sea snake is shiny and yellow with dark green bands.

SNAKE FAST FACTS

Length: 3 feet (1 m)

Food: Fish and shellfish

Found: Indo-Pacific Ocean

28

SNAKE BITE

The Belcher's sea snake can hold its breath for up to 8 hours while hunting or sleeping.

Latin name: *Hydrophis belcheri*
(say it like this: hi-DRO-fiss bell-KIR-eye)

Fer-de-lance

- The Fer-de-lance is nervous, unpredictable, and strikes swiftly and aggressively.

- Fer-de-lance hunt at night.

- The Fer-de-lance is gray or brown with black-edged diamonds in lighter color.

- The rainforest's moist environments are the Fer-de-lance's favorite spots.

SNAKE FAST FACTS

Length: 4 feet to 7 feet (1.2 m to 2.1 m)

Food: Small lizards, centipedes, rodents, frogs, and other snakes.

Found: Central and South America

Latin name: *Bothrops asper* (say it like this: BOTH-rawps ASP-er)

Boomslang

- The boomslang has beautiful green scales with black in between and a yellow belly.

- Boomslang live in trees.

- It glides through the tree branches when hunting.

- Boomslang have large eyes with excellent eyesight.

- A boomslang has 1/8-inch to 1/4-inch (.3-cm to .6-cm) rear fangs. They are located in the mouth beneath the eyes.

SNAKE FAST FACTS

Length: 4 feet to 6.5 feet (1.2 m to 2 m)

Food: Birds, lizards, insects, and sometimes other snakes

Found: Trees of sub-Saharan Africa

A Boomslang can open its jaw to 170 degrees when striking. That is almost straight up and down.

Latin name: *Dispholidus typus*
(say it like this: diss-FOHL-ee-dus TIE-fiss)

Gaboon Viper

44 lbs

- The Gaboon viper has the longest fangs at 2 inches (5 cm).

- This snake waits for its prey to come to it.

- A Gaboon viper has a pale body with tan markings, which is excellent camouflage.

SNAKE FAST FACTS

Length: Up to 6 feet (1.8 m)

Food: Birds, rodents, rabbits, and insects

Found: Central and southeast Africa

The Gaboon viper is the heaviest **venomous** snake in Africa. It can weigh up to 44 pounds (20 kg).

Latin name: *Bitis gabonica*
(say it like this: BIT-iss gab-ON-ih-ka)

Eastern Coral Snake

- Coral snakes are slender with a rounded nose and similar looking tail.

- When threatened, a coral snake will sometimes make a popping sound.

- Coral snakes have bright-colored bands of red, yellow, and black.

- There are 85 species of coral snakes in the world.

- Coral snakes are nocturnal.

- A coral snake has highly **toxic venom** but very small fangs. It holds onto its prey to **inject** the **venom.**

SNAKE FAST FACTS

Length: 18 to 36 inches (46 to 91 cm)

Food: Lizards, frogs, and other snakes

Found: North, Central, and South America

The coral snake is a cousin to the cobra.

Latin name: *Micrurus fulvius*
(say it like this: mi-CREW-russ full-VEE-uss)

37

Water Moccasin

- When frightened a water moccasin will curl into an S-shape with its head back and mouth open to display the white inside.

- The colors of a water moccasin vary from dark brown or black to olive. Their bellies are pale.

- Water moccasins swim on the surface of swamps, marshes, ditches, ponds, lakes, and streams.

SNAKE FAST FACTS

Length: 2 feet to 4 feet (.6 m to 1.2 m)

Food: Fish, small mammals, birds, amphibians, lizards, baby alligators, turtles, and other snakes.

Found: Southeastern United States

SNAKE BITE

The water moccasin is also called a cottonmouth because of the white color inside its mouth.

Latin name: *Agkistrodon piscivorus*
(say it like this: agg-KISS-tro-don pisk-EE-vor-uss)

Eyelash Viper

The eyelash viper has scales over its eyes that look like eyelashes.

Eyelash vipers spend their lives in the trees and shrubs of tropical rainforests.

Eyelash vipers can see really well.

The eyelash viper comes in many colors including red, brown, yellow, green, and pink.

SNAKE FAST FACTS

Length: Up to 2.5 feet (.8 m)

Food: Small mammals, birds, lizards, frogs, bats, rodents, and **marsupials**

Found: Central and South America

Eyelash vipers have a **prehensile** tail to move around in the trees just like some monkeys.

Latin name: *Bothriechis schlegelii*
(say it like this: bo-THREE-kiss SHLEG-ell-ee-eye)

Burrowing Asp

- There are 19 species of burrowing asp.

- The burrowing asp has large fangs for a small snake

- A burrowing asp attacks sideways.

- This snake injects venom deeper because of its saber-toothed fangs.

- This brownish-pink snake lives in underground burrows.

SNAKE FAST FACTS

Length: 20 inches (51 cm)

Food: Rodents, reptiles, frogs, locusts, and ants

Found: Southern Africa and Middle East

The teeth of a burrowing asp stick out of its mouth. It can bite without opening its mouth.

Latin name: *Atractaspis*
(say it like this: a-TRACK-tasp-iss)

Reticulated Python

- A reticulated python can weigh as much as 350 pounds (159 kg), almost as much as a male sheep.

- The reticulated python is the world's longest snake.

- Reticulated pythons do not have any **venom** and rarely bite. They are dangerous because they get so big and heavy.

- The reticulated python is an excellent swimmer.

SNAKE FAST FACTS

Length: 10 feet to 20 feet (3 m to 6 m)

Food: Rodents

Found: Southeast Asia, **invasive** in the southeastern United States

Reticulated pythons wrap their bodies around their prey and squeeze.

Latin name: *Python reticulatus*
(say it like this: PIE-thon reh-TICK-u-lah-tuss)

Green Anaconda

Green anacondas like to be near or in the water.

Green anacondas are not **venomous**.

A green anaconda can measure more than 12 inches (30 cm) around.

Anacondas live in swamps, marshes, and streams.

SNAKE FAST FACTS

Length: 15 feet (4.6 m)

Food: Fish, birds, tapirs, wild pigs, capybaras, caimans, and sometimes jaguars

Found: South America

A green anaconda is the heaviest of all snakes. It can weigh as much as 550 pounds (250 kg).

Latin name: *Eunectes murinus*
(say it like this: YOON-eck-tess mur-IN-uss)

Glossary

carnivore – an animal that eats the flesh of other animals

carrion – dead or rotting flesh

cold-blooded – having blood that changes with the temperature of the air or water

deflate – to cause to shrink or collapse by letting out air or gas

extinct – no longer existing

fossils – the remains or a trace of a living animal from a long time ago

herpetologist – a scientist who studies reptiles, including snakes

hollow – having an empty space on the inside

inflate – to make larger or expand by letting in air or gas

inject – to put into by force or pressure

invasive – does not belong in the habitat where it is found

marsupials – an animal group that includes kangaroos and opossums

pit – a sense organ that helps snakes hunt in darkness by detecting body heat.

poisonous – filled with or containing poison

prehensile – adapted for seizing or grasping

toxic – containing poison

unhinge – to remove something from its hinges in order to open wider

valves – the part that controls the flow of a liquid or gas

venom – a poison that some animals produce, including snakes

venomous – producing venom